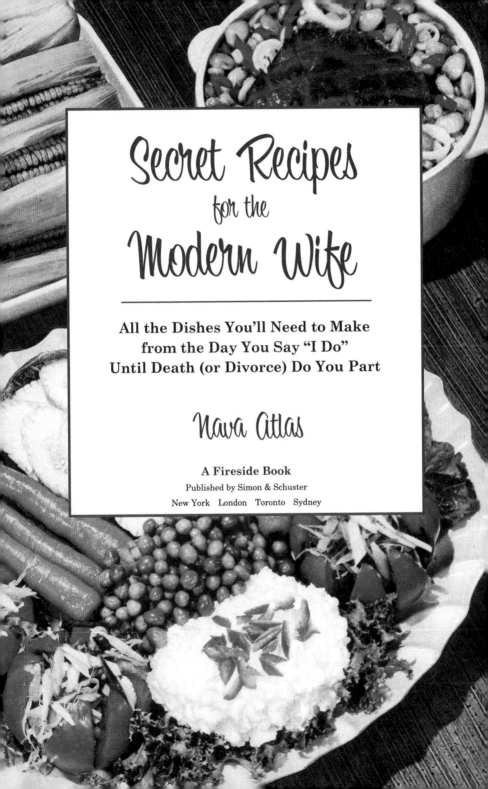

Secret Recipes
for the
Modern Wife

**All the Dishes You'll Need to Make
from the Day You Say "I Do"
Until Death (or Divorce) Do You Part**

Nava Atlas

A Fireside Book
Published by Simon & Schuster
New York London Toronto Sydney

Fireside
A Division of Simon & Schuster, Inc.
1230 Avenue of the Americas
New York, NY 10020

First Fireside trade paperback edition April 2009

FIRESIDE and colophon are registered trademarks of
Simon & Schuster, Inc.

For information about special discounts for bulk purchases,
please contact Simon & Schuster Special Sales at 1-800-456-6798
or business@simonandschuster.com.

Designed by Nava Atlas

Manufactured in China

1   3   5   7   9   10   8   6   4   2

ISBN-13: 978-1-4165-8084-3
ISBN-10:   1-4165-8084-0

Contents

Jim's late for dinner . . . again!

Introducing the Recipes

Whether you're a new bride or an old hand at marriage, a collection of fresh and fascinating recipes to add to your repertoire is always welcome. And the recipes in this collection are perfect for you, the busy, overextended, and occasionally conflicted modern wife. Enveloped in them are the secrets—delicious, distressing, and everything in between—that accompany women on their marital journeys.

Here are recipes you won't find in just any cookbook. As a young wife and mother, you may favor dishes that are as accommodating as you, like Gender Role Casserole and People-Pleasing Tossed Salad (though you'll eventually gravitate to Way Too Much on Your Plate). A few years into marriage, some restlessness and conflict may arise, making "recipes for trouble" mighty appealing. Sample some Beans 'n' Weenies of Sexual Tension, Old Boyfriend Buffet, or Midlife Stress-Stuffed Cabbage.

If yours is one of the 50 percent of marriages that end in divorce, well, you've still got to eat. Choose from an array of dishes that will leave just the bitter aftertaste you'd expect; Grounds-for-Divorce Meat Loaves and Psychotherapy Pie are just two of the recipes for disaster that will serve you well. For dessert, though, be sure to indulge in Sweet Cakes of Hope.

Finally, our recipes for reconciliation and romance are sure to please those who've found contentment and, yes, even happiness, as they've weathered the joys and challenges of family and married life. Even if you've gotten burned on the stove of marital strife, however, these recipes just might inspire you to find someone new and give it another go. So, get comfortable, pour yourself a cup of coffee or tea, and browse through these secret recipes. Some are delectable, others lamentable, but you're sure to find favorites to serve again and again.

Part One

Recipes for Accommodation

Start your marriage right by pleasing
your man, your kids, and everyone else
with these tantalizing treats

Sweethearts' Engagement Buffet

Serves 1 newly committed couple
and their guests

6 cups all-purpose societal and cultural expectations
Generous slab of prenuptial bliss and relief
1 overflowing case of sugarcoated wedding fantasies
Butter for tenderizing
Maraschino cherries for topping
Daisies for decorating (but not for eating)

In a big mixing bowl, combine expectations with the first blush of engagement and relief that you can quit the hellish dating scene forever.

Cream together with wedding fantasies, gathering everything you've gleaned from novels, magazine articles, and the wedding (but not the marriage) of Diana to Charles, along with every Julia Roberts and Meg Ryan movie you've ever watched. Marvel at how rapidly you've been transformed into the kind of bride-to-be you swore you'd never become.

Use as much butter as needed to grease your fiancé's ego, proving he has chosen wisely by choosing you. Suppress those parts of your personality that are ambitious, aggressive, and abrasive. Display only the juicy, fruit-sweet side of you that still believes that life is a bowl of maraschino cherries.

Scatter a myriad innocent white daisies over the buffet table. For now, ignore any trepidation you may harbor about making marriage last a lifetime. After all, you've got a wedding to plan, with mountains of details and major expenses to manage before that one perfect day. You'll have plenty of time to deal with the actual marriage when the time comes.

Honeymooners' Bountiful Brunch

Serves 1 hungry couple

2 generous handfuls of lust, or enough to obscure
  rational thought and sensible decision making
6 cups novelty, or as needed
Small dollop of reality
Drizzle of domesticity
Blueberries
Toasted crushed walnuts
Cornmeal
Pure maple syrup

Preheat lust until nearly too hot to handle, then cover until it has cooled down enough for you to realize that desire alone is not enough to sustain a relationship (though it can often make it more agreeable).

Sprinkle in an abundance of novelty, using enough to keep your level of tolerance high when you begin to realize that your new husband's quirks are, well, *quirky,* and not as charming as they seemed before the wedding. Look at him lying next to you, snoring, and think, This is it? Forever? Wonder whether he belched this much, or snorted in his sleep, when you were dating.

Once the reality sinks in that this is really it, resolve to make your domestic arrangement as cozy as possible, even though when you were a type-A student, or fiercely focused on your profession, you didn't give a flying fig about cooking, cleaning, or decorating.

Keep some coffee as well as your relationship percolating as best you can, and when novelty is reduced by half, fold in some yummy ingredients like blueberries, walnuts, and cornmeal. Shape into muffins, biscuits, waffles, and coffee cake. Come on, you can make this work—he's still hungry, and you are, too. Sweeten with lots of syrup.

Shrimp Cocktail with a Rather Disappointing Sauce

Serves 1 no-longer-newlywed couple

Sauce
1 scant cup disenchantment
2 heaping tablespoons finely diced restlessness
Handful of issues, left unresolved
1 teaspoon hot paprika
1/4 teaspoon cayenne pepper

2 dozen fresh jumbo shrimp, still exuding optimism

In a nonreactive saucepan, combine disenchantment and restlessness. Heat gently until they bubble to the surface. Analyze why you often feel this vague sense of malaise—shouldn't you be happy? After all, you're *married*. But it's not nearly as exciting as the chase was, and certainly not as exciting as planning the wedding.

Sprinkle in all the issues you chose to underplay or ignore when you were dating: trust issues, money issues, control issues, dependency issues, codependency issues. Not to mention religion, children (whether to have them, and how many), and family (yours and his). Season with paprika and cayenne, cover, and allow the sauce to ferment for up to two years.

Just before serving, taste the sauce to make sure it's not too spicy or bitter. Steam the shrimp, then let cool and arrange on a bed of green ice.

Puncture the shrimps' optimism slightly with a toothpick or other sharp object. Dip into the sauce and consider whether, given all the lingering issues, the dish meets your expectations (which, like the shrimp, are jumbo), or whether you aren't just a tad disappointed.

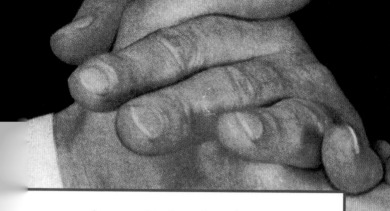

What a Turkey Noodle Soup

Serves 1 finicky spouse

1 fussy eater, who shall remain nameless
1 former yogurt eater—guess who?
1 quart of quandaries about nightly dinner decisions
Low-level resentment, stirred up, about why said
    dinner decisions are suddenly the primary domain
    of aforementioned yogurt eater
Canned, convenience, frozen, and takeout foods

Admit that in the early days of your relationship, you glossed over how particular your significant other could be about food. Reminisce about how easy it was when you just had yourself to please: yogurt and berries for dinner, or lo mein noodles straight from the carton—yum!

Uncork your quart of quandaries: contemplate why suddenly, it almost automatically falls to you to plan, shop for, and make dinner. Ask yourself: "What is this—the fifties? Am I supposed to magically morph into June Cleaver?" When really tired and hungry, wish you'd married one of those guys who love to cook.

Put a temporary bandage on the problem by stocking up on lots of premade foods. Vow that once you have a family, you'll make healthy meals from scratch. Oops, you better run—the microwave is beeping.

Gender Role Casserole

Serves 1 resentful mom

1 adult female, probably you
1 adult male, presumably your husband
Children, as planned or who just happened
Hard-boiled egg wedges and sliced olives for garnish

Combine yourself with your husband. When you are fresh from the altar, swear you'll never fall into stereotypical gender roles. Allow yourselves to marinate until you've spawned some children.

Perform the following functions: boo-boo kissing, tummy ache rubbing, temperature taking, nose wiping, all school-related stuff (field trip chaperoning, teacher conference going, lunch making or lunch money giving, homework supervising, bake sale baking, etc.), car pool organizing, play date arranging, playground going, appointment making (doctors, dentists, haircuts, music lessons, etc.), meal planning, food and clothing shopping, social organizing, form filling, summer camp arranging, laundry doing, bed making, snack preparing, party giving and going, gift buying, and on and on until you're ready to puke.

Observe your husband at the following: spending increasing amounts of time at work and/or work-related travel, becoming inordinately interested in sports or the Internet, performing occasional minor house repairs, emptying the garbage, and taking sporadic care of the children.

Complain that said husband promised to be an equal partner in domestic duties, upon which he patronizingly explains that since he is earning more money, you should logically take on most of the household and childcare duties. Wonder how you turned into your mother (or grandmother, if your mother was part of feminist movement). Arrange eggs and olives over the top.

You've always wanted kids . . .
Well, now you've got 'em!

How will you feed
a family, when
you can barely
make a decent
dinner for yourself
and Hubby? And
those dishes!
He'll promise to
help with cleanup,
but don't expect
miracles.

Be prepared to serve
your children des-
peration dinners far
more often than you
intend. This toddler,
for example, has
been served a whole
quail and a square
egg by her exhausted
mother.

Quick! If you make a meal while no one is watching, you can pretend you've made it from scratch!

And now that you've got 'em,

You've gotta feed 'em!

You'll frequently do your grocery shopping on the run, without a list or a plan. You won't be proud of it, but, once in a while, your shopping cart will look just like this: filled with packaged foods, with hardly a hint of fresh produce!

Way Too Much on Your Plate

Serves 1 frazzled female

2 to 3 small children, or more or less, as desired
Small pinch of time
1 large bunch mixed obligations (try a combination
    of work, aging parents, extended family, community
    involvement, and endless errands)
Generous grindings of guilt

Combine children in a house or apartment and stir together, losing temper every so often.

With time at a premium, pile up obligations and to-do items, little by little, until you realize that you have so much on your plate that your life resembles one motley potluck. With a wire whisk, beat yourself into stiff peaks for biting off far more than you can chew.

Add as much guilt as necessary to achieve complete emotional overload when you realize that there is no way to do anything well when you are trying to do so many things at once. Ponder why your life, which was relatively simple not long ago, has become a not-too-pretty smorgasbord.

Start recipe over each morning and repeat daily for about a decade, or longer as needed, until the kids are older or until you are a complete basket case, whichever comes first.

No one tells you . . .

How much children change a marriage!

See how your new Modern Maternal Feelings change your core identity and outlook and how they irrevocably alter your marital relationship!

Admit it. You've always wanted to be a mommy. But your notions of motherhood came straight from ads featuring fat, bouncing babies and cinematic or sitcom children—those sage, charming mini-adults, always far wiser and saner than the actual adults around them. Sure, most men say they'd like to be dads. In truth, most guys would rather get a new car than have a child.

No one tells you how hard it is to be a parent. No one tells you how much children change your marriage. Shock sets in when you discover that real kids are nothing like the ones in movies or on TV. Sometimes they are so unlike you that you wonder if they have been dropped from another planet. They have needs. They have issues. They require all manner of extremely expensive equipment and services.

Yet once these crying, puking, needy beings enter your life, you're hooked. How you feel about Hubby pales in comparison with your overwhelming love for them. Everything they say is adorable, everything they do an amazing act of genius. There is nothing you wouldn't sacrifice to make their lives more fulfilling.

Make modern motherhood gratifying by going with the flow of your newly emerging feelings and emotions. Accept that, for some time, nothing will be the same. Later on, the essential "you" that gets submerged will resurface, and you may even rediscover your hubby—that's a promise!

People-Pleasing Tossed Salad

Serves you more generously than you'd like

1 bushel of everyone else's needs, your own
    needs picked over and discarded
Untold hours of catering to your children and husband
Requests for volunteer duties and personal favors
    that you just can't seem to refuse
1 small jar of capers, drained
Plenty of oil
Not too much vinegar—it will give you heartburn

Tend to everyone else's needs, gently and lovingly at first; then, when you start to come to a simmer, stew in the repressed rage of your own resentment.

After several years of waiting on your family hand and foot, wonder why you didn't set firmer limits, and let everyone learn to do things for themselves.

Ask yourself why you always seem to get sucked into so many unappreciated tasks and projects (and what you may be avoiding or distracting yourself from) and why you are too wimpy just to say no to requests to do favors for everyone under the sun.

Combine all of the above in the salad bowl of life; add the capers, oil, and vinegar and toss well. Eat a large helping as you ponder why you've become so self-sacrificing, and why your own needs seem to matter so little to you.

This salad makes a huge portion that no one else will want to share with you, so be prepared to have leftovers—alone—for a long time to come.

Good cooks are
GIVING THEIR HUSBANDS CHOICES!

Smart wives follow these simple rules:

✔ **GIVE HIM CHOICES, PLENTY OF CHOICES!** Even if you just open cans, make sure he gets to choose from at least three varieties of soup, for example, and at least five kinds of sandwiches.

✔ **SERVE ALL HIS OPTIONS AT THE SAME TIME!** Men need to be able to spread their choices out, and see them all at once. They pride themselves on being "big-picture people."

✔ **HE CAN "HAVE HIS SOUP, AND EAT IT, TOO"!** Serve him all three soups at once, or one at a time. He can sip or slurp, and he can eat his sandwiches before, with, or after the soup. He can sip or slurp, and he can run around the table between bites, if that's what he chooses to do.

✔ **TAKE YOUR PICK, MA'AM!** You, on the other hand, must limit your choice to one kind of soup and one type of sandwich. Sorry, but women still need to make choices that men never have to think about.

Part Two

Recipes for Trouble

Long after the glow of marital novelty has
worn off and life's unrelenting challenges
set in, these morsels will hit the spot

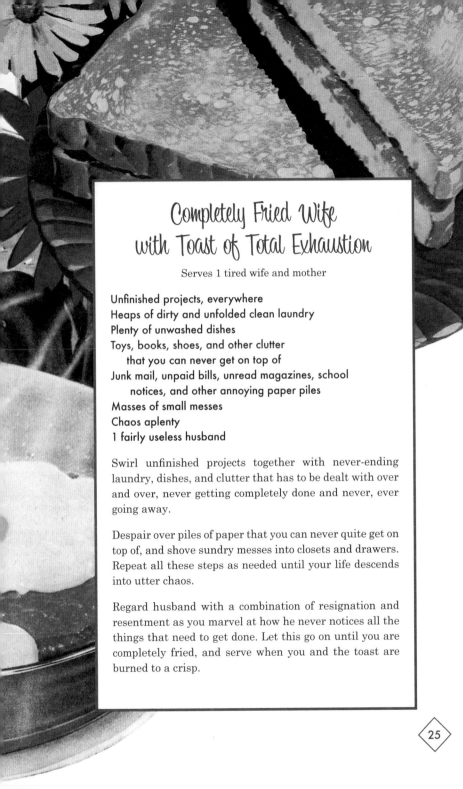

Completely Fried Wife
with Toast of Total Exhaustion

Serves 1 tired wife and mother

Unfinished projects, everywhere
Heaps of dirty and unfolded clean laundry
Plenty of unwashed dishes
Toys, books, shoes, and other clutter
    that you can never get on top of
Junk mail, unpaid bills, unread magazines, school
    notices, and other annoying paper piles
Masses of small messes
Chaos aplenty
1 fairly useless husband

Swirl unfinished projects together with never-ending laundry, dishes, and clutter that has to be dealt with over and over, never getting completely done and never, ever going away.

Despair over piles of paper that you can never quite get on top of, and shove sundry messes into closets and drawers. Repeat all these steps as needed until your life descends into utter chaos.

Regard husband with a combination of resignation and resentment as you marvel at how he never notices all the things that need to get done. Let this go on until you are completely fried, and serve when you and the toast are burned to a crisp.

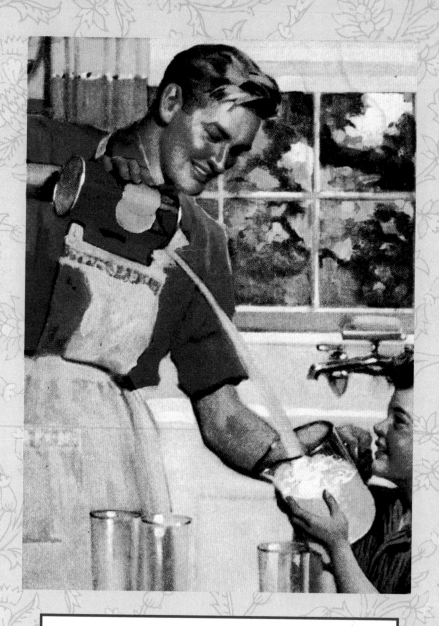

When hubby offers his assistance, try to be appreciative. Come on, you know what I mean. You're always kvetching about how you'd like him to do more with the kids and to help with household tasks, but when it comes right down to it, you find it difficult to let go.

He tries to help, but you can't help micromanaging: "No, not THAT way!" See how helpful Dad is, teaching Junior how to get grapefruit juice into a pitcher from a severe angle two feet away. Don't be like this wife, who pretends to be pleased but is actually horrified.

Beans 'n' Weenies of Sexual Tension

Makes enough to muddle your love life

Abundance of mismatched sexual needs
Countless incidences of feigned desire
Nearly as many incidences of feigned sleep
Generous portion of rote sex with little affection
Big chunk of mind-numbing monogamy
1 can baked beans, warmed
Sliced pumpernickel bread, as needed
Tomatoes, lettuce, and radishes
Corn relish

Place in a grinder in order as follows: all the times when he wants sex and you don't; the nights when you're hot to trot and he has no interest; all the occasions that you gave in to him when you were tired, upset, or just plain bored; all the times that you pretended you were already asleep so that you could avoid having sex; and your resentment at being an object of sexual gratification without any attendant affection or intimacy.

Cut in a chunk of ennui caused by going to bed with the same person, night after night, year after year.

Grind until finely chopped, then stuff into casings to create your own hot homemade weenies. Sauté until lightly browned, then serve piping hot with beans, fresh pumpernickel bread, salad vegetables, and corn relish. Yummy!

Incredibly Expensive Skirt Steak

Serves 1 overextended family

Barbecue sauce
Unaffordable mortgage
Rapidly rising property taxes
An extravaganza of insurance (home, life, health, auto)
Home repairs and furnishings
Child care and/or tuition
Clothing, entertainment, frivolous purchases, etc.

1 bloody, overpriced raw slab of steer
Pineapple rings for topping

Combine the ingredients for the barbecue sauce in a savings or checking account and mix together. Realize that there is not nearly enough to marinate the meat. Take the meat and throw it on a grill topper.

Have a rip-roaring argument over important expenses as well as frivolous purchases. Make sure to criticize each other's "money style." Arrange pineapple rings fetchingly over the surface of the problem, then grill.

Banana and Sweet Potato Tango

Serves the 2 who are doing the tango

1 medium or small (ha!) banana
1 lovely sweet potato

Cut the banana and sweet potato any way you wish, but recognize that no matter how you cut them, even in this day and age, the banana's job, opinions, and preferences almost always take precedence over the sweet potato's.

Mother-in-Law Fruitcake

Serves your hubby and his mom, for whom
no one (least of all you) will ever be good enough

2 cups all-purpose flour
1 to 2 cups chopped nuts—the more nuts, the better
1 tablespoon leavening
Cool disapproval masquerading as politeness
Appalling behavior
Snide remarks and gossip
Interference
Unsolicited opinions
1 pound candied fruit, or enough to cover the
    bad taste left from the 5 previous ingredients

In a big mixing bowl, make a dough that's as nutty as your MIL deserves it to be. Stir up until you can cut the tension with a knife, then add the leavening to diffuse the situation.

Fold the following ingredients into the dough: mom-in-law's forced politeness, which doesn't fool you for a minute (she's never really approved of you); her unpredictable behavior (no one in *your* family would ever act like such a drama queen); a liberal dose of insidious, snide remarks and gossip meant to subtly needle you; interference with how you raise your kids and run your home; and plenty of unsolicited opinions, especially about religion and money. Cover up the bitterness with lots of candied fruit.

Pour the mixture into a loaf pan and bake until a knife inserted into the center pierces her pompous pride. Slice and serve with accusations that your hubby, "the prince," is too spineless to set boundaries and doesn't stand up for you when you've been slighted.

Go out and buy yourself a box of fine chocolates with which to console yourself, because no one, least of all you, really likes fruitcake, anyway.

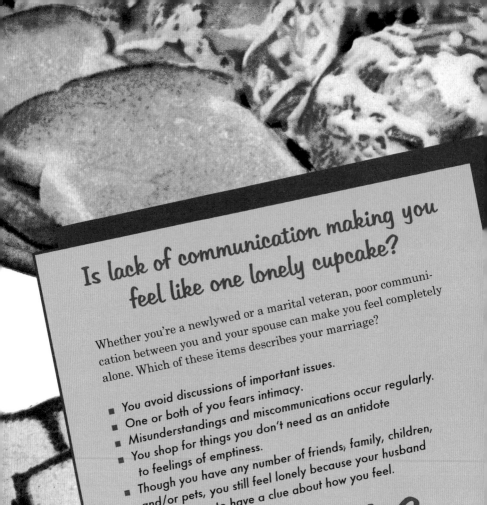

Is lack of communication making you feel like one lonely cupcake?

Whether you're a newlywed or a marital veteran, poor communication between you and your spouse can make you feel completely alone. Which of these items describes your marriage?

- You avoid discussions of important issues.
- One or both of you fears intimacy.
- Misunderstandings and miscommunications occur regularly.
- You shop for things you don't need as an antidote to feelings of emptiness.
- Though you have any number of friends, family, children, and/or pets, you still feel lonely because your husband doesn't seem to have a clue about how you feel.

What to do?

Either gather up your courage and work at those communications issues or, better yet,

AVOID THEM!

Just as you can avoid home baking from scratch, you can sidestep the important issues in your marriage by sweeping them under the rug. Doing so will probably come back to haunt you in years to come, but why worry about it today? You'll deal with your snowballing problems later (or not). Now, go and treat yourself to something starchy or sweet.

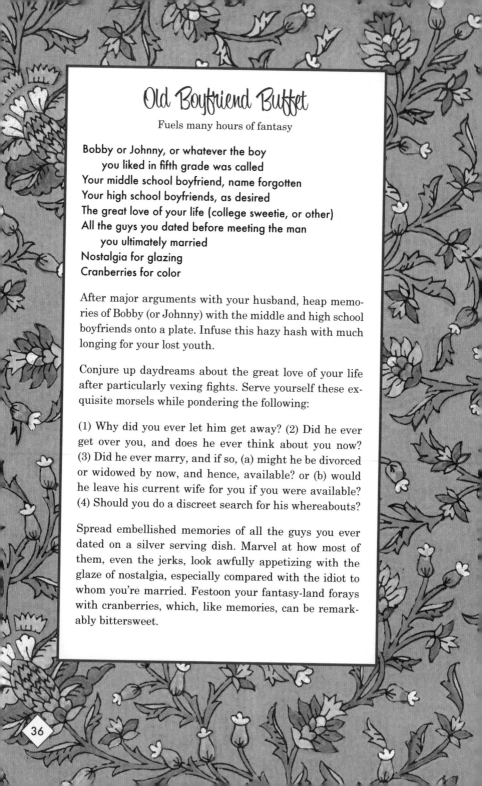

Old Boyfriend Buffet

Fuels many hours of fantasy

Bobby or Johnny, or whatever the boy
    you liked in fifth grade was called
Your middle school boyfriend, name forgotten
Your high school boyfriends, as desired
The great love of your life (college sweetie, or other)
All the guys you dated before meeting the man
    you ultimately married
Nostalgia for glazing
Cranberries for color

After major arguments with your husband, heap memories of Bobby (or Johnny) with the middle and high school boyfriends onto a plate. Infuse this hazy hash with much longing for your lost youth.

Conjure up daydreams about the great love of your life after particularly vexing fights. Serve yourself these exquisite morsels while pondering the following:

(1) Why did you ever let him get away? (2) Did he ever get over you, and does he ever think about you now? (3) Did he ever marry, and if so, (a) might he be divorced or widowed by now, and hence, available? or (b) would he leave his current wife for you if you were available? (4) Should you do a discreet search for his whereabouts?

Spread embellished memories of all the guys you ever dated on a silver serving dish. Marvel at how most of them, even the jerks, look awfully appetizing with the glaze of nostalgia, especially compared with the idiot to whom you're married. Festoon your fantasy-land forays with cranberries, which, like memories, can be remarkably bittersweet.

Control-Freak Cookies

Makes just as many as your husband wants you to make

Ingredients for cookie making (flour, eggs, butter,
    sugar, cocoa, nuts, raisins, etc.)
Generous fistful of your husband's insecurities
Matching amount of your own vulnerabilities
1 big bunch of his inability to trust that anyone
    else (aside from himself) can do anything right
Neurotic perfectionism
Red and green sprinkles

Arrange baking ingredients on the counter as neatly as possible for fear that your husband will walk into the kitchen and begin rearranging them even more neatly himself.

Take pity on him for a moment, if you can, realizing that his raging insecurities and anxieties are what cause his neurotic need for control and order. Let the moment pass. Well, that's just tough—you have your own vulnerabilities to deal with.

And while you're on the subject, why can't he trust that you can accomplish things on your own, without sticking his nose into everything? Why does he always have to be in the driver's seat (literally and figuratively), and have the last word on every decision, large and small? Why does he get to decide how many cookies you make, and what kind? Why does he think that *everything* is *always* about him?

Arrange the cookies on platters, as neatly and symmetrically as you can, in order to avoid yet another hassle with the crazed perfectionist. Garnish some cookies with red and green sprinkles, making sure to wipe up any that fall on the table. Serve immediately with good, strong coffee (but let him make the coffee—he doesn't think you make it strong enough).

Midlife Stress-Stuffed Cabbage

Serves 1 couple until they go completely mad

2 sets of aging parents, rapidly deteriorating
1 to 3 wiseass teenagers, or more in blended families,
    growing up alarmingly fast
Escalating auto insurance rates
Way too many college applications at any given time
Inadequate college savings accounts
Life-sucking jobs—his, yours, or both
Enough wisdom to recognize all the
    mistakes you've made over the years
Not enough wisdom to correct them
Large cabbage leaves, as needed
Olives, peppers, debt, and despair for topping

Combine the first 8 problems (and you can use up any others that are rotting in your pantry). Pulverize into a pounding headache.

Stuff the cabbage leaves and, while performing this tedious task, think about doing rebellious things you did when you yourself were a wiseass teenager, like getting some extra piercings or hitching a ride to Guatemala.

Top with olives, peppers, debt, and despair and bake until everything and everyone has a complete meltdown. Serve with a flaming temper.

Bland, Boring Bean Pots

Makes an unrelenting amount

10 pounds of practically flavorless white beans
1 economy-size can of everything you
   and your husband ever had in common, drained
Colander of conversations, strained
Overflowing cauldron of nearly identical days
Flagon of familiarity
Smidgen of molasses
Random, unrecognizable items for topping

In a Dutch oven over a low flame, combine the beans with the following elements that make your marriage if not terrible, then, frankly, pretty unexciting: the reality that you and your husband no longer have much in common; your strained conversations (especially when it's just the two of you—alone—at the dinner table or in a restaurant); and days melting into more days that are practically indistinguishable from one another.

Infuse the entire enterprise with a big splash of familiarity (which, as Mark Twain attested, breeds contempt—and children). Taste, and adjust the practically nonexistent flavor of this dish with a bit more of each ingredient until there's way too much of it, yielding enough leftovers to last for years.

In a halfhearted effort to perk up the flavor, dribble in some rich, dark molasses. If that doesn't do the trick, top each portion with something, anything, even if you can't quite figure out what it is, just to give yourself the sense that you're doing *something*. Serve in front of the TV, yawning profusely, and fall asleep after taking a few bites.

Part Three

Recipes for Disaster

If you're on the road to Splitsville,
here are some dishes that will leave you
feeling disappointed, angry, and betrayed

Whoosh! All those years
you devoted to this
sham of a marriage—gone!

Whoosh! The ambitions
and goals you've long
cherished—unfulfilled!

Whoosh! Daring dreams of adventure and world travel—too late now!

Whoosh! Your youthful energy and fresh looks —down the toilet!

Hypercritical Cinnamon Buns

Makes a seemingly endless supply

Dough
Plethora of petty complaints directed by your husband
      at poor, unappreciated you
Slew of withering criticism of you, usually unfounded

Filling
1 cup raisins
1 teaspoon cinnamon (or substitute cyanide)
Myriad criticisms (mostly well deserved)
      you lob at your husband, but only when
      you're really frustrated

Powdered sugar for glazing

For the dough, knead the petty complaints together with the often unfair complaints you must endure at the hands of your husband (you either don't make enough money, waste money, are a money-obsessed workaholic, or don't make *any* money; spoil the kids; spend too much time on your looks or not enough time on your looks; don't pay enough attention to *his* needs, blah, blah, blah).

For the filling, pound the raisins and cinnamon (or cyanide, for a spicier effect) with the things you criticize him for, like his sloppiness (i.e., wet towels and dirty clothing and socks everywhere), unfinished house projects, not helping enough with the kids, getting absorbed with his hobbies while you don't get a single minute to yourself, how his drinking is getting just a tad out of hand, letting his parents and siblings get away with murder, his potbelly, etc.

Put the filling in the dough and go round and round the same subjects ad nauseam. To temper the critical flavor of the buns, top with a generous powdered-sugar glaze.

Soufflé of Fallen Expectations
Makes 1 collapsed endeavor

8 large eggs, separated
3 pounds of long-standing myths about marriage,
    derived from film, fiction, and women's magazines
Several drops of strawberry-flavored essence
1/2 cup heavy cream, or enough to make you
    feel fat and guilty
1/4 cup sugar
Disillusionment, as needed

Separate the yolks from the whites of the eggs, just as now you are finally separating fantasy from reality. Throw the yolks away, then regret wasting them.

Whip the whites into a frenzy, then stir in all the myths you've acquired about marriage from childhood on up to the present moment. Gently fold in the realization that most of these cultural narratives are fictions. Add the strawberry flavoring to forestall the taste of inevitable disappointment, along with the cream and sugar. Bake in a hot oven until the soufflé is inflated beyond reasonable expectations.

Remove from the oven and watch as the soufflé deflates. Allow yourself to feel disillusioned—men really *are* from Mars, and women from Venus, and never the twain shall meet.

Begin to recognize that for all the effort you put into this dish, there isn't much to show for it. Decide whether it's worth trying to salvage the soufflé as well as your marriage, or better just to throw the whole thing away.

Broiled Sacrificial Chicken

Serves a small crowd of defeated wives

4 small plump broiling chickens, well rinsed of
   salmonella bacteria
8 ounces each: insecurity, wishy-washiness,
   and possible loss of independence
3 things you really want to do, but are afraid to try
3 experiences you truly crave but deny
2 teaspoons coarse salt
1 cup finely crushed hopes or cornflakes,
   or half of each

Rip the thighs and wings off the poor chickens. Rub your insecurity, wishy-washiness, and loss of independence into their thin skins.

Make a marinade of all the things you've long wanted to do but for which you lack the courage, and the experiences you've always craved but somehow manage to repress.

Let all your wants and cravings marinate into the skin of the chicken. Do your best to ensure that all of it remains just under the surface, so that you can forestall making any changes in the status quo for as long as possible.

Roll the chicken parts in salt and crushed hopes and/or cornflakes and broil the hell out of them.

Shop wisely! Shop for flavor!

Trusting your husband

should be as easy as opening a can of peas.

Unfaithful Meatballs

Serves 1 philandering bastard

2 to 4 years of suspicious or provocative behavior
    (looking, flirting, prolonged absences, etc.)
1 jumbo package of clever lies and near misses
Sluts, as bastard desires, probably as stupid
    and gullible as you are, or more
Cell phone calls, e-mails, and bogus
    business dinners, as needed
Business trips, real or fake, optional
1 can green sugar peas

Ignore or rationalize, as best you can, suspicious behavior, past and present. What the hell are you supposed to do, with children still at home? Maybe it's nothing; maybe your imagination is overactive.

Then again, maybe he is just as double-crossing, nefarious, deceptive, and manipulative as you suspect. In that case, combine lies, sluts, phone calls, e-mails, so-called business dinners, and optional business trips. Notice that bastard's cell phone is always turned off during latter two. Shape into balls while entertaining thoughts of exacting revenge. Fry in hot oil.

Cook the already overcooked peas until they are as wrinkled as his disgusting toes. Admit that this is one of the worst recipes ever. If you can possibly forgive him for forcing things to come to this, try counseling. But if this meal is beyond your ability to digest, arrange his perfidious meatballs on a plate and tell him that if he doesn't like them, you're out of here.

Unsalvageable Coconut Cake

Makes 1 very messy situation

1 heaping helping of issues that often feel
    insurmountable
1 last-ditch effort at counseling
Quivering package of trepidation about the future
1 heaping cup fear of the unknown
1 case of nerves about how to tell the kids
1 teaspoon each: vanilla, almond, and
    butterscotch extract
2 cups shredded coconut

Bring your issues into the open with the assistance of
a counselor. Let them air out. Once it seems clear that
this effort is fruitless, face your trepidation and fear. (Is
being single really preferable to toughing this out? How
will you make it on your income, or lack thereof? How
will you pay the mortgage? Will he at least shell out for
child support? Yikes!)

Stir in a case of nerves (What should you actually say
to the kids? Will they understand? Who will they want
to live with?), working into a froth, or until completely
coagulated.

Stir the vanilla, almond, and butterscotch extracts into
the mix in a last-ditch effort to salvage it (at least it will
smell better), then cover with the shredded coconut.
Form into a lumpy mess; bake until devoid of any hope.

Acknowledge that this cake, like your marriage, is not
very pretty, resembling nothing more than a desiccated
meat loaf wearing a dirty blond wig. Heave a big sigh,
and begin to accept the inevitable. Steel your nerve and
serve with a glass of chocolate milk and divorce papers.

Grounds-for-Divorce Meat Loaves

Serves 2 people who have gone in separate directions

4 pounds of continually rehashed beefing
1 big smack of realization that you've really
    changed—or is it he who has changed?
23 annoying habits
8 pairs of dirty socks
Pointless arguments, as needed
Steamed brussels sprouts and carrots
Bizarre vegetable garnishes
2 mediocre attorneys

Throw all your complaints and incompatibilities into a large mixing bowl and go over and over the same issues until you're completely worn out.

Hit your forehead with the wooden spoon of fate as you discover that one of you has changed—is it you, or him? It hardly matters any longer.

One by one, toss in the habits you found so charming in the beginning but which now just annoy the hell out of you. Pick his socks up just one last time from the floor, and toss those in, too. Shape into two separate lives— that is, loaves—and bake until you've taken just as much as you can.

Surround the loaves with brussels sprouts and carrots, then get the jerk into the kitchen and see who can outdo the other with outlandish garnishes, odd behavior, and unreasonable demands. Once the two of you determine that you can no longer negotiate this contest on your own, call in attorneys to be the judges.

Psychotherapy Pie

Makes 1 swell 9-inch pie

1 flaky 9-inch piecrust

Filling (use any three or more)
Canned fruit of your choice
Self-doubt
Low self-esteem
Anxiety
Anger
Denial
Low-grade depression

The best therapist you can afford

For the crust, use all the compensatory or addictive behaviors you've developed over the years to shield yourself from your true feelings.

Combine the canned fruit with any of the relevant filling ingredients and pour into the crust. Stand there dejectedly, feeling yourself at a crossroads.

Once you realize you can't deal with these damned pie fillings by yourself, seek the help of a therapist. Discuss filling ingredients with the therapist until you arrive at the best way forward, or until you come to the conclusion that you are better off without all the stuff in this pie. Consider making a healthy salad, instead.

61

Sweet Cakes of Hope

Serves 1 newly single female

Generous handful of good friends
Supportive family members, as needed
Several fine imported revelations
Large pinch of insightful self-awareness
1 pound of courage, or more, as needed
1 bottle self-worth, preferably extra-virgin
3 packages cake mix
1 half-gallon carton positive outlook
Lots of new possibilities for icing

Gather up your friends and family, and rely on them as much as they've relied on you over the years.

Mix the revelations and insights you've arrived at during this difficult period of self-search with all the courage and self-worth you can muster.

Combine in a mixing bowl with cake mix (hey, you've got lots to do right now, and don't have time to make all these cakes from scratch). Add some positive outlook—after all, you're over the hard part, and can now begin to see that you can go on without someone who was, let's be honest, dragging you down. Put into as many pans as you'd like and bake until huge and fluffy and as close to perfect as these cakes can get for now.

For the icing on the cake, spread with lots of interesting new possibilities you never would have considered before. As the old saw goes, have your cake and eat it, too. Eat lots of it. After all, now you need no one's permission but your own.

Part Four

Recipes for Reconciliation and (Gasp!) Romance

If your marriage has had more ups than downs, and you're in it for the long haul, serve these cozy dishes for pleasure and sustenance

The best husbands are like good corn—

ESPECIALLY IF THEY'VE GOT THESE TRAITS . . .

Tenderness

If you're sick, he'll take care of you. If you're sad, he'll make you laugh. He'll buy you thoughtful gifts and be kind to your family. Like a well-cooked corn kernel, he's tender and sweet.

Maturity

The best corn is picked when it's perfectly ripe. Don't pluck a man off his stalk before he's ready, or you'll be waiting forever for him to grow up and assume responsibility.

Consistency

A good husband is as consistent and dependable as the uniform kernels in a fresh ear of corn. Your marriage should not blow with changing moods and whims. You can count on him!

Endurance

Like love, corn is sweetest when young; with care, it can last for a long time. You can't can or freeze your man, but if you're kind to each other, you may go the distance.

Is your marriage in the doldrums?

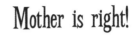

Mother is right!

How do you think she's managed to stay with your dad for so many years? When you experience a relationship's ups and downs, as you're bound to (even in the best of marriages), smooth things out with warm, creamy tapioca. Tapioca pudding will:

✛ Foster greater understanding between you and your husband

✛ Recharge your sense of togetherness and revitalize your sexual chemistry

✛ Improve communication, and help build understanding of each other's needs

✛ And, best of all, help him to recognize and appreciate all that you do for him.

——— ———

Make some tapioca pudding today! Put the mmmmmmm back in your marriage!

Sometimes I Feel Like a Tart

Serves its purpose once in a while

Passion, revisited
Sex, for comfort and relaxation
Sex, for healing
Sex, for love and affection
Sex, for mood therapy
Sex, just for its own sake

Recall the early years of your relationship, when you brought unbridled passion to a rolling boil, then tasted and savored often. Ruminate on the manner in which passions cooled gradually during the next few years, at which point you set them on a low, steady flame to help keep your marriage moist and tender.

With passions now at room temperature, indulge in sex (a) to lull yourself into a comfortable stupor or as a way to relax; (b) as a means of making up after arguments; (c) to remind yourself—or to create the illusion—that you're still in love and can give and receive affection; and (d) to tame the testosterone tiger—men are definitely less edgy after a roll in the hay.

Despite tepid passion, serve up a portion of piping hot sex as often as you possibly can—it's a small island of bliss within the vast sea of life's despair.

Crispy, Savory Contentment Casserole

TIRED OF CONFLICT AND DRAMA in your daily repertoire? Keep your recipe for marital contentment simple! All you need are a few key ingredients that are probably already in your pantry:

- ✔ A mellow filling consisting of understanding, perseverance, maturity, and mutual nurturing

- ✔ Crispy, crunchy elements (choose from among self-development, shared adventure, continued education, or potato chips), to keep things interesting

- ✔ A tasty topping to make everything go down easily

Your first bite might seem less than exciting, but after letting it linger on your palate, contentment usually creeps in, accompanied by the comforting flavor of long-term attachment.

You may need to make this dish a few times to work out all the kinks and get it just right, but if you persist, you may even experience moments of true happiness.

73

A Fairly Satisfactory Family Stew

Serves those who can endure the effort of preparation

2 large tear-inducing onions, finely chopped
Effort, as required
Olive oil
Ambivalence, as it arises
1 large pinch of perspective
Family-size package of patience
Love, as needed
Biscuits for added coziness

While chopping the onions, weep a few tears of frustration as you exert the effort required to cook this complex stew of family life—the one you've created with your partner and the families you joined together.

Ask yourself if you're up to the task of doing the hard work involved in concocting a flavorful, functional family stew, or if you want to continue your life as an aging party girl or an arrested adolescent.

Inhale deeply the savory scent of the onions as they cook in olive oil, becoming less bitter and stinging, and far sweeter and softer with time. As your weeping subsides, acknowledge lingering ambivalence about some of your main ingredients (including your husband, and even your kids, who might actually be more palatable if they were breaded and baked).

With a good pinch of perspective, come to accept that it can be quite satisfying to weather the peaks and valleys of seeing through such a challenging recipe, and that with patience, it may yield many tasty meals for years to come. Allow the stew to bubble along for as long as need be, and serve by the ladleful with love and biscuits.

He sometimes does the dishes and laundry

I don't have to deal with the kids alone

Mrs. F. W. Frankel says: "I don't know about all this talk of men and women being equal. I sure wouldn't want to get stuck mowing the lawn, tarring the roof, and decapitating the chickens, would you?"

Mrs. Elmer Davis agrees: "My Elmer takes out the trash, shoos varmints away from the house, and keeps my feet warm at night. He's a good father, and he don't drink too much or snore too loud. There ain't too many like him out there, I tell you."

"Why would I want to start over again at my age," asks Mrs. John Yoder, "when I've got a perfectly good husband at home? The grass isn't always greener, you know. If you're feeling a bit restless, take up a hobby, like skeet shooting."

He does a lot of the taxes

He's like a portable space heater

He's a pro with a snowblower

He deals with leaks and electrical problems

takes out
e trash

Some Benefits of Preserving Your Marriage

or, don't give up before you've given it half a chance

77

So they
lived happily
ever after

Happily-Ever-After Ambrosia

Serves to inspire hope in an age of cynicism

The stuff that makes marriage most delectable (choose as many as you'd like), including:

    Shavings of fresh coconut
    Harmony
    Pineapple rings and candied fruit
    Affection and mutual respect
    Glistening cubes of ruby red gelatin
    Security and support
    Mint ice cream
    Children who turn out well
    Rich frosting and whipped-cream toppings
    Lasting love and happiness
    Chocolate syrup (lots of it)

Before starting this recipe, recognize that even in an age when impossible standards of perfection coexist with a decline in marital rates (and successes), there must be *some* reason why most people aspire to be part of a committed couple.

While arranging delicious ingredients with lofty aspirations, pause to reflect on "for better or worse" and decide that you prefer better. And observe that even those who have endured the most painful of breakups often try again (and sometimes yet again).

Realize that real life doesn't always resemble a dessert buffet, filled with sensuous pleasures and emotional fulfillment. Still, it's human nature to feel hopeful, and even though you know that "happily ever after" exists primarily in fairy tales, it may be possible to grab morsels of love and happiness from time to time.

Acknowledgments and Credits

This book started its journey as a personal project (a small, limited edition artist's book) in response to the fact that several of my friends were going through the turmoil of divorce or marital malaise at the same time. They shared their woes with me and did not mind one bit when their tales were cooked up into "secret recipes." On the contrary, the stories of strife were so universal that seeing their shared experiences emerge as dark humor seemed cathartic. Those who experienced the most painful breakups were those who, oddly, found the most hilarity in the early version of this project.

I'd like to thank this group of women, dear friends whose names I'll leave out, though they know who they are. I so appreciated your enthusiasm and your encouraging me to expand the original into the full-fledged book that it has become.

Trish Todd, my editor, saw beyond the divorce theme of the original work and suggested that this book could be about all aspects of marriage, not just its discontents. With a light hand, Trish helped shape this book into a more balanced picture of contemporary marriage, including its sweet aspects as well as its challenges. As an editor and colleague, she is a treasure. Thanks also to all those at Touchstone Fireside who have been involved in bringing this offbeat book to fruition.

There are not enough effusive words in the English language to do justice to my agent, Lisa Ekus, and her associate, Jane Falla. I'll keep it simple and say how very grateful I am that these remarkable women are part of my life, and I hope it will be so until death do us part!

I had long wanted to integrate my art and publishing paths but wasn't sure how to do so until I returned to earn a master's degree as an older student. And the person most responsible for helping to achieve my goals is Ann Lovett, who as my professor and thesis adviser pushed me far beyond my self-imposed limits. I doubt I would have even thought of the idea for this project had I not taken her inspiring book arts class.

Finally, my husband of many years, Chaim Tabak, deserves

profound thanks. I kept reassuring him, "Honey, this book is *not* about you," as it was taking shape, and it's true. He has always been my biggest fan and supporter, no matter how quirky or complicated a venture I undertake. I hope that our marriage and life with our sons, Adam and Evan, can always aspire to be like the one in the last recipe of this book, Happily-Ever-After Ambrosia.

I wish to thank the following companies for permission to reprint images in this book as follows:

Bon Ami Company, for images used on pages ii and 65.
The Great Atlantic & Pacific Tea Company (A & P) for images on pages 13 and 49.

Campbell Soup Company for images used on pages 9 and 20–21 (photos copyright Campbell Soup Company).

Massimo Zanetti Beverage USA for images on pages 46–47.

Pabst Brewing Company, for the image on the Contents page.

State of Florida, Dept. of Citrus, for the image on pages 26–27.

J.B.S. Swift & Co., for black-and-white images on pages 20, 76, and 78.

About the Author

Nava Atlas is the author and illustrator of many popular vegetarian and vegan cookbooks, including *Vegan Express, The Vegetarian Family Cookbook, The Vegetarian 5-Ingredient Gourmet,* and *Vegan Soups and Hearty Stews for All Seasons.* Her award-winning Web site, In a Vegetarian Kitchen (vegkitchen.com), is one of the most widely visited vegetarian/vegan venues on the Web. Nava never imagined that she would produce a book that contains so many images of meat. In truth, there is likely not a single dish in this book she would actually consume, though, metaphorically speaking, she has partaken of Gender Role Casserole more often than she'd like to admit.

Nava is also an active fine artist (navaatlas.com) specializing in text-driven art and limited edition artist's books. Her artwork is in the collections of many museums and universities in the United States and abroad. She lives in the Hudson Valley region of New York State with her husband and two sons.

Index of Marital Dishes and Dramas